THE BOOK OF WEALTH

Prophet Salem Ephias

The Book of Wealth

Salem Ephias Publishing
Rebirth Nation

A CIP catalogue record for this book is available from the British Library. This publication employs archival quality paper.

ISBN: 978-1-908552-83-9

The Book of Wealth

Prophet Salem Ephias

Table of Contents

Introduction

This comprehensive guide delves into the intricate realm of wealth, offering profound insights and revelations on the art of acquiring abundance. The Book of Wealth serves as a roadmap, providing deep insights into the principles that govern the accumulation of wealth.

The significance of cultivating a strategic mindset is a central theme, acknowledging that many individuals yearn for wealth yet struggle to attain it despite fervent efforts such as fasting, prayer, and financial investments. This book addresses the fundamental failure to recognize the true value of money and presents strategies to unlock the right value that leads to success and access.

Within these pages, the role of angels in facilitating financial breakthroughs is explored, emphasizing the importance of understanding our dominion power in summoning wealth. Various postures and positions that enable access to wealth are unveiled, offering readers a holistic approach to wealth acquisition in diverse dimensions.

The Book of Wealth is a practical guide, equipping readers with strategies to attain wealth in different facets of life. It goes beyond conventional wisdom, unlocking revelations that propel individuals to higher dimensions in their finances, business strategies, and overall life navigation towards prosperity.

Key concepts are highlighted to align readers with divine ordinations, challenging and reshaping mindsets to facilitate access to the wealth predestined for each individual. This book serves as a transformative tool, urging readers to reconsider their thoughts and conduct in daily life as they embark on a journey towards the wealth that awaits them.

Chapter 1:

History of Wallstreet 0.1

According to Britannica, Wall Street is commonly known as the Financial District. It is the southern section of the borough of Manhattan in New York City, which has been the location of some of the chief financial institutions of the United States. The street is narrow and short and extends only about seven blocks from Broadway to the East River. It was named for an earthen wall built by Dutch settlers in 1653 to repel an expected English invasion. Even before the American Civil War, the street was recognised as the financial capital of the nation.

Its name means wood and war. In the 1700 it became the main hub of trade for the whole world. Therefore, you can't talk about wealth without referring to Wall Street. The financial crisis that took place in the world all happened within the walls of Wall Street being that the world's money is governed by it. However, it was originally built to protect the Dutch.

In Ecclesiastes 7:12 (KJV) "For wisdom is a defence, and money is a defence: but the excellency of knowledge is, that wisdom giveth life to them that have it," there are two things that are a defence, wisdom, and money. During the period of the 1653s and the 1700s the identity of Wall Street transformed. As a result, it is not a coincidence that persons who protected themselves due to the war by building a wall in a certain place, the name and place are carried on and it becomes a hub (the effective centre of an activity, region, or network) of money not long after. With Wall Street being incorporated in these two aspects, what is taking place? They are trying to show you that money is a defence.

Vulnerability vs Confidence

Although money is a defence another aspect of money can be seen through personality which can be in a state of confidence or vulnerability. Vulnerability can be determined whether or not you lack money. Insecurity often arises from a sense of lacking, and this is frequently observed, particularly among men, where the deficiency is commonly associated with financial limitations. Everyone who was introverted or shy when they were younger, the moment, they had money their persona changed, and they became extroverted due to money becoming their defence. The defence causes your state of mind or awareness to change which allows you to ignore criticisms and can operate in confidence due to the security money guarantees. Another scenario is that it allows you to make confident decisions without the influence of others, however, those with brilliant ideas who lack money are usually very hesitant/shy in presenting their ideas.

Value of Money

Money is not defined as a physical thing or by an amount, it is the mindset that you have. You can have a dollar, but its value differs depending on who possesses it. For instance, consider a scenario where you enter a restaurant, retrieve a dollar, hand it over, and leave. Now, imagine the President of the United States entering the same establishment, pulling out the same dollar from his pocket, and presenting it. In this case, the restaurant owner would likely hold the President's dollar in higher regard. The owner might go on to frame the dollar, signifying the memorable occasion. Hence, it is your thought patterns that determines the value of the money you possess; it is not the money itself that enhances your value. This distinction is often overlooked by many. If money is still adding value to you, you still have a poverty mentality because a rich mindset adds value to money.

Creating Value

Matthew 2:11 (KJV) spoke about the wise men coming from the East, bringing valuable gifts to give to the Lord Jesus when he was a baby who could not even speak. It is because they knew the value that he had as he was the one who was adding the value to the gifts, not vice versa. When they thought of the Lord Jesus the first thing that came to their mind was, "What is it that we can give to him?" They are not looking at their gold being the one that is adding value to him but they are looking at the value that he has and asking, "What is it that can at least match up to the value that he carries?" So, whenever people think about you what value do they see in you? In today's society, it is advocated to be yourself, but your appearance can reduce your value, people get to understand and know us based on what we have given to them or what we show them. So, what side of you have you shown?

Value is established through the image you project, rather than the quantity of possessions you hold. This image has the potential to instil trust, which serves as a distinct form of defence. For instance, consider a situation where you possess all the necessary resources and ample funds for a business investment in a specific location. Despite having solid proof, the absence of perceived value diminishes trust, hindering potential business transactions.
Conversely, in a different scenario, an individual may have cultivated trust by building personal value, even if they lack immediate financial resources. In such cases, they may secure a slot or opportunity without the immediate need for financial commitments.

Jesus created value by telling His people that they didn't need any gold, any purse, or any money with them because they already had enough value to sustain themselves. The understanding that we have is that whenever you have a mission the first thing that you are talking about is a budget to execute the mission, but Jesus is telling the disciples to not carry any money at all Mark 6:12-13 (KJV), he's trying to say that they now have enough value.

To gain value you have to rewire your mindset. The secret to succeeding is being strategic about your marketing or strategic about your positioning. There are four "Ps" that are fundamental elements of marketing; product, place, price, and promotion (packaging). There are questions that you should focus on when being strategic. How are you packaging it (it has to do with marketing strategy)? How are you pricing it? How are you positioning it (where are you selling it?)

Strategy to Prosperity

Many stores strategically cause people to spend more than they intended. It is very difficult to spend the exact amount in a supermarket because the essential products that people need daily are not found at the front of the store, for instance, milk, cereal, and bread. They are all positioned in places where you must travel through other products to get them then on your way back you have to see other products. Another strategic position is at the check-out station, at this place you are waiting to buy your items. The human mind is programmed to do something; therefore, we cannot be idle. An idle person is not someone who is motionless but is someone who does things that are not productive and do not give or add any value. The purpose of the queue in supermarkets at the check-out station is to cause a delay so that the products displayed can capture a person's mind to release them from boredom with the aim that they are idle enough to put the small, hand-picked items into their cart. They also strategically place candy in that area if the parents are not influenced, the children will persuade them so by the time they are at the counter they will have more than they anticipated.

We fail to learn from our environments or how they function when it is based upon strategy. Being disciplined allows you to be intentional which causes you to be able to budget and prevents you from overspending. However, possessing money as a defence will cause you to view this as unproblematic. A mindset of prosperity allows you to strategize on who you associate with and how you conduct yourself which adds value to you. In Proverbs 23:1-2 (KJV),

"When you sit to dine with a ruler, note well what is before you, and put a knife to your throat."

A person can respect you based on your communication skills because words can hinder you from benefitting from the access that you have been given at that table. It is important to consider who you are speaking to because you cannot speak to everyone the same. A great or successful person gives you access, not because they just want to spend time with you, they aim to study you, therefore, be a person of a few words. A wise person will make you feel comfortable enough that it will cause you to lower your guard to allow you to speak without caution; the freedom that you were given is to test your character and this is how many fail before successful people. A successful person is someone who can give you access to something that you need. It could be a security guard, that is the one that has the access that you need.

Success is all about strategy, a picket fence with a beautiful house, and your dream car is not the definition of success, but it can be the destination. Success refers to the implementation of the process that is used to achieve the goal.

Hype vs Success Theory

Hype is not success it is the shadow of success. The Hype season is a preview, or the demonstration of what success looks like. Its purpose is to show you how achievable success is and set as a reminder that you need to put in the necessary work to receive the actual success permanently. Many people settle for the hype season which is temporary and when faced with difficulties they are seeking to go back to the hype season. The process consists of the hype season being on one end and then the horrible season being the bridge success on the other end. The level of determination or effort that you have will dictate the level of your achievement.

These success codes consist of four words:

1. Organization- An organization is like an association in an institution. Allocate people to positions within the institution. This also includes those who surround you.

2. Perfectionism- Failures do something until they get it right, successful people do something until they can't get it wrong.

3. Diligence- Be consistent and persistent to the point of being willing to leave yourself behind if you are the one who is stopping your progress.

4. Prudence- Be disciplined enough that you don't need anyone to remind you to get things done.

Chapter 2:

Angel of Wealth: Understanding the role of angels in your life

In the realm of the spirit, angels are known as ministering spirits created by God to serve as divine messengers. They follow God's commands and are bound by His will. It's essential to comprehend the significance of God's word in your life to instruct your angels. Unfortunately, many people fail to do so and end up giving verbal commands to their angels without understanding God's word over their lives.

When you're protected by angels, it's because God has already dispatched them for your protection. According to scripture Psalms 91:11-12 (KJV), there are angels of protection who prevent accidents and near misses from occurring. These angels are an integral part of God's plan to keep you from harm and prevent you from falling.

It's important to note that angels will not do anything outside of God's will, even if you command them to. Knowing God's word concerning your life is the key to instructing your angels. This is why the devil attempted to test Jesus by tempting Him to throw himself down, not realising that he was speaking to the creator of the angels. Matthew 4:5-7 (KJV)

Accessing the angels of wealth

John 20:1-18 (KJV)
Luke 7:37 (KJV)
John 12:1-8 (KJV)

You'll read about Mary going to the tomb. When she got there, she did not see anything because she did not look. She only saw it was empty and she didn't stoop low to see what was inside. She just saw the stone that was covering the tomb was rolled away and it looked empty, so she ran back to speak to Peter and John. When she reported it, they left and they went and those guys were the ones that stooped in to see what was happening. They only saw linen there; nothing else and they went back.

Upon Mary's return, she carefully looked. When she did this, she saw two angels, one sitting at the feet and one at the head where the body of Jesus had lain. Now imagine, as spiritual as John and Peter were, they were the same men Jesus chose to take to the mountain where He transfigured and where they saw Elijah and Moses in the flesh. The two disciples are failing to see the angels because they were in the tomb and were not assigned to Peter or John, they were assigned to Mary. For this reason, her prophetic connection, whilst Jesus was alive, she came and broke an alabaster box jar filled with expensive perfume worth about a year's wages. She broke it at the feet of Jesus then anointed His feet, she also used her hair to wipe His feet, the same point of the connection she used is the same point of connection the angels are coming to reveal themselves to her.

So when Mary goes back to the tomb, to use her hair and anoint His feet, her point of connection and sowing is the same way the angel of prosperity appeared to her.

The question arises, if Mary had seen an angel, how did she fail to recognise Jesus with whom she had walked in the flesh before with? She already knew Jesus' appearance and voice and had experienced His presence before His death. So, if Jesus was the one, she encountered, why did she not recognise Him? How did she have the spiritual eyes to see two angels but neglect to see Jesus?

It's worth noting that the two angels were assigned to Mary, but Jesus was not resurrected to appear to her. Instead, He was resurrected to appear to His disciples, which is why He instructed Mary to inform them. Mary's encounter was with the angels of wealth, who do not move as one. Therefore, that exact point of connection is significant. Mary anointed Jesus' feet and wiped them with her hair, which made her cry. Her tears activated the angels, leading to the revelation.

If you receive a message through meditation and feel led to sow a seed, the same meditation will activate the angels of wealth. Similarly, if you experience joy and gladness in your spirit, that same joy will bring back the angels of wealth. However, when accessing the realm of angels, it's essential to remember that the way you enter is the same way you should revisit. It's like a house with doors. No matter how big it is, the doors that are initially put in place are the same doors that you will use. Therefore, when you activate the angel of prosperity, the way you access it is the same way you should re-enter. Mary had the keys to the angels of wealth, which oversee ensuring that the report of your seed, sacrifice, and offering is taken to the Lord. This is why every time the gospel is preached, there's mention of an offering. Mary unlocked this revelation.

It's essential to understand that you cannot access something through an entrance you didn't create. You must activate and access a realm through its corresponding entrance. It's only inside a realm that you can create a new entrance. This idea is echoed in the story of Mary's encounter with Jesus, where her revelation came from the angels and not directly from Jesus. Similarly, there are certain angels, such as the angels of wealth, that can only be accessed at specific times, such as early in the morning when it's still dark. Those who are truly committed to prosperity and success recognise the importance of waking up early and seeking God's blessings at the right time. The story of Jacob in Genesis 32:24-28 (KJV) highlights this point.

Jacob received his father, Isaac's blessing, but it didn't manifest until he wrestled with an angel at Bethel. The angel was fighting to leave before light came, showing that it was still very early in the morning. Jacob's persistence in wrestling with the angel was not in vain and he received the blessing he had been seeking.

It's crucial to understand that success and prosperity require dedication and a willingness to seek blessings at the right time. Just like creating an entrance to a realm, you can't access a blessing through an entrance you didn't create.

Jacob was blessed and given the name Israel; an identity that represented a nation destined for prosperity. It is through this identity that they are bound to thrive. Interestingly, men access the angel of wealth through wrestling while women do so through positioning. Mary was an example of the latter, while Jacob was an example of the former.

The Importance of Staying Alert in Life's Seasons

The Book of Proverbs offers some valuable insights into the perils of indolence. Proverbs 6:10-14 (KJV) highlights how a lack of diligence can lead to poverty and unexpected wants. Laziness can rob us of opportunities, and we may not even realise it until it's too late. Proverbs 19:15 (KJV) emphasises how idleness can lead to hunger, causing us to miss out on important teachings and opportunities.

While rest is crucial, it's also important to recognize when to take it. Even our physical bodies know when to rest, and so should we. Prioritising rest is essential, but if we rest our entire lives, we may end up toiling in our old age. It's crucial to be mindful of when to rest and when to seize opportunities. After all, we don't want to look back and regret all the missed chances.

In Matthew 13:25 (KJV), the Bible discusses how sleeping can lead to the enemy sowing tares among the wheat. It is crucial to understand the different levels of life, particularly when sowing and harvesting. When building your wealth, for instance, you are still at the sowing stage and must remain vigilant. You only rest when you have harvested and secured your bounty. The field is an open ground, and seeds are sown without security; thus, it is essential to stay awake and attentive. Even when sowing a seed, the devil may also attack by sowing his own seed. For instance, when sowing a seed for prosperity, the devil may plant one for unemployment. Therefore, you must remain alert in all aspects of life as you never know where the enemy will strike.

Promotion and prosperity often happen when people are asleep. Mary Magdalene, for example, woke up early in the morning while it was still dark. Similarly, Jacob wrestled with an angel before sunrise, fighting for his prosperity. There is a time to sleep, but you must maximise strategic moments to gain success. Markets operate when people are asleep, and they predict outcomes before they happen. You must be wise to this and not miss opportunities.

In conclusion, it is essential to stay awake and alert in different seasons of life. Always remember that there is a time for everything, and maximizing strategic times is crucial to success.

Men Wrestle & Women Position

Proverbs 31 outlines a woman who is a leader in her home. She rises early to provide for her household and assigns tasks to her maids. She equips herself with spiritual, mental, and physical fitness to perform the God-given task. Are you following her example? Do you rise early to take care of your household and equip yourself? It takes strength and discipline to live up to this standard.

Many women focus on the part of the scripture that describes them as precious and valuable, but fail to follow the Proverbs 31 example. Your value is not measured by words alone, but by your actions. Do you challenge yourself mentally, spiritually, and physically? Do you work out and engage in activities that promote your overall well-being? These are the things that define a Proverbs 31 woman.

The woman at the alabaster box had to work to get it. She didn't just wake up one day and see it manifesting. You must do the same. Don't just talk about your value, live up to it. Start by praying, reading, and challenging yourself mentally and physically. Only then can you truly call yourself a Proverbs 31 woman.

It's no secret that men and women have different approaches when it comes to accessing the angel of wealth. Men often must wrestle and toil, cursed to till and sweat the ground, while women position themselves for success.

For women, hard work and dedication can lead to a successful outcome, whether in fitness or any other endeavour. Men, on the other hand, must break their backs and fight for their success.

However, it's important to note that only those with the motivation and strength to fight can access this realm of wealth. Professional fighting is a prime example of this - the risk and training involved yield great rewards for those who persevere.

In conclusion, both men and women can find success in accessing the angel of wealth, but it requires different approaches. Women can position themselves for success with hard work and dedication, while men must be prepared to fight and take risks. Either way, success is within reach for those who are determined to make it happen.

Chapter 3:

Unveiling Financial Success Through Vision and Faith

The concept of financial freedom goes beyond merely having money. It is freedom from being governed by money. Drawing upon Luke 16:13 (KJV), Jesus explains this by stating that it's impossible to serve two masters. This implies that one may either dedicate oneself to a particular pursuit or divide their attention, leading to dissatisfaction in either case. Money is comparable to a master; it has the power to control and dictate one's life. In our world, there are numerous entities that can govern us. Still, money stands out; it holds a powerful influence which can equal and surpass other influences, potentially even the one exerted by God. In this context, it's important to note that God and money are similar. Both are influential forces that can address our needs and wants. Yet, to secure any kind of financial stability, one needs to have a clear vision, not simply aspirations.

The Bible advises us to concretise our vision by writing it down, to share it and inspire others Habakkuk 2:2 (KJV). Let's consider Matthew 16:4 (KJV), where it says, 'A wicked and adulterous generation seeketh after a sign; and there shall no sign be given unto it, but the sign of the prophet Jonas.' We should ponder upon the meaning of 'sign.' A sign refers to a miracle. According to this passage,

Jesus qualifies as 'wicked and adulterous' those who relentlessly pursue miracles. Possibly, you might be someone who's counting on God to perform a miracle. God declares such a pursuit as wicked and adulterous. But let's not misconstrue the term 'wicked.' 'Wicked', in this context, is not indicative of evil. It stems from the Greek word 'Poneros,' meaning 'full of labour, full of toiling.' For instance, your regular nine-to-five job could be what evokes a perceived need for a miracle.

Labouring excessively due to a lack of vision is the sentiment here. When there is a clear vision, there's a precise direction. A firm vision guides you, by charting a direction, and helps you work smartly instead of simply working hard. Let's consider an instance from the Bible where Peter, despite toiling the entire night, was unable to catch any fish. Jesus instructs Peter to cast the net back into the sea. Why should Peter follow the advice of a stranger? Should he believe that merely by throwing the net back, he would catch something despite a previous unsuccessful attempt? On Jesus's suggestion, Peter cast his net again and had the most significant catch of His life. This transformation occurred due to two reasons: firstly, the authority of Jesus's words and secondly, his foresight. Peter's assumption was that the fish would be near the surface at night. But fish, as living creatures, can decide their own location. Thus, Peter required someone with prophetic insight, not just assumptions based on natural patterns.

Often, our misconception is that money resides within occupations, whereas it truly lies within visions. You may assume that working a regular nine-to-five job guarantees financial security. However, if your goal is solely monetary without a discernible vision, you will find that money evades you. Clear vision and direction are key, not labouring aimlessly in search of wealth.

Genesis 47:14 (KJV) recounts how Joseph gathered all the money in Egypt and Canaan during times of famine and used it as a tool to fulfil needs. Financial prosperity merely isn't about accumulating wealth because money can fail.

True prosperity is inherent, as exemplified by Joseph who was prosperous while being a slave. Prosperity resides not in physical possession but within oneself. Joseph's vision made him the 'go-to' person during famine, while Pharaoh was the actual ruler of Egypt. When you possess a vision, people who are failing financially start to seek you out because what they need isn't money but a solution, which lies in your vision.

Always remember, money seeks solutions because money tends to flow where there's a need.

To communicate your vision to others, you need to be clear and authoritative in your communications. This will encourage others to heed your instructions. Just like Joseph, through perseverance, positioned himself as the governor of Egypt, you can create a path for success through your vision.

Thwarting financial lack ultimately depends on understanding the problem and offering the right solution, not merely seeking the money. Vision is not merely seeing things; it involves living them. People aren't able to perceive the vision you've penned because you're still viewing it instead of living it. You don't need money to possess something. It's about knowing that something belongs to you and boldly claiming it as yours.

God has plans to prosper you, but it requires your active involvement. Miracles aren't about sitting idle but working towards making them happen. It is not necessary to have wealth to feel a sense of ownership. When you fully understand and accept that something is meant for you, it truly belongs to you. Assess what you truly need and what you merely desire, and assertively claim those requisite things as your own. According to principles, when you anticipate a blessing, it implies that there is an existing divine plan for you. Blessings do not miraculously appear out of thin air; there is a careful creation and organisation behind them. Take an active role while waiting for the miracle to unfold. Don't remain idle but give it your effort and energy.

Many people command angels to gather wealth and deposit it in their bank accounts. "I command you to pay my rent now." The psalmist indicates that angels follow God's orders, carrying out tasks based on His ultimate will. Failing to understand God's will prevents the ability to command one's personal angels. As believers guided by the Holy Spirit, it's our responsibility to provide direction to our angels. They don't instruct or lead us. However, the challenge is that the plans and what you need is known only to God. Therefore, one must strive to access this divine knowledge. This is why it was said, "No eyes have seen, no ears have heard...," but through the Spirit, we comprehend God's thoughts. God has promised, "I have plans to prosper you and not to harm you." But where could we find these plans? They are revealed in God's mindset. So, what is God's mindset? It is essentially the Spirit.

Remember, faith directs you towards your own success and not others'. It may give no tangible proof, but it always produces evidence. Surrendering to the illusion that wealth is not meant for you is a defeatist mentality. Successful outcomes demand patience and unaverred commitment towards your vision, just like Abraham who waited for 99 years for his promised son, Isaac.

To summarise, financial prosperity is not merely about having money—it's about having a vision. Your vision will direct you towards your financial goals and create opportunities for income. It's important to highlight the distinction between vision and sight. Your vision is your future reality, not just an abstract idea. Vision is not only seeing something; it is being able to live in it. You are not yet benefiting from your vision because you are still seeing it rather than living it.

Hence, before seeking financial miracles, create a vision.

Do not seek temporary solutions; instead, focus on the vision God has given you. This does not mean waiting idle for a miracle to happen, but rather actively participating in the manifestation of that miracle.

Remember, you do not necessarily need money to feel the ownership of something. If you truly believe something belongs to you, then it does. You must command the resources you need and want, considering them as your rightful possession.

Finally, be patient and develop resilience in your pursuit because only then can you achieve your true destiny. Remain focused on the vision given to you, regardless of the obstacles you face or the suffering you must endure. Remember, it's often necessary to endure the challenges life throws your way to shape your destiny and realise your vision.

Chapter 4:

The Distinction Between Wealth and Money

Although wealth and money may seem indistinguishable, they are two distinct concepts.

Wealth is a dimension, a realm that contains the spirit of money. In the same way that Earth is a realm containing human beings that are both flesh and spirit, wealth is a dimension containing the spirit of money. The heavens too have their own spirits, as mentioned in Ephesians 6:12 (KJV).

While wealth is a dimension, money is a spirit that dwells within it. There is no scripture that compares Jesus to wealth, nor is there any scripture that associates wealth with evil or wrongdoing.

Money, on the other hand, is often mentioned in scripture. As Jesus said in Matthew 6:24-26 (KJV), a person cannot serve both God and mammon (money). One cannot be enslaved by money.

The Bible has a lot to say about money, including 1 Timothy 6:10 (KJV) which suggests that the love of money is the root of all evil. Similarly, in Matthew 6:24-26 (KJV), God is defined as spirit and those who worship Him must do so in spirit and in truth. These verses emphasize the importance of recognizing that the love of money is a spiritual issue, not just a financial one.

God's love is associated with purity and is unconditional. Even when we are lost, God loves us and sacrifices His son to save us. Similarly, when we love money, we do so in the same way - unconditionally and with everything we have.

It's important to differentiate between want and love. While everyone needs money to some extent, it's not because we love our jobs so much. We need money to meet our basic needs, such as having a place to stay. Money becomes an exchange for these needs. Money is a spirit and wealth is a dimension.

In the context of Deuteronomy 8:18 (KJV), the word "power" is translated from the Hebrew word "Koch", which means "ability" or "strength" inspired by the Holy Spirit. This divine ability to get wealth is a process that involves divine intervention. While people may earn money, they may not necessarily acquire wealth. The ability to generate wealth is a dimension where individuals can manufacture or create money instead of simply earning it.

It's important to note that earning a salary alone won't make anyone a millionaire. Rather, individuals need to have the ability to generate wealth. This ability is bestowed upon them by the Lord, and it's crucial to remember and acknowledge Him in this process.

Deuteronomy 8:18 (KJV) emphasises the importance of divine ability in generating wealth. It's not just about earning money, but rather about creating and manufacturing wealth in a dimension where individuals can generate money.

You can have wealth and not have money. Peter met Jesus, and Jesus told him to follow Him and He would make him a fisher of men. Matthew 17:24-27 (KJV) Jesus is giving Peter this instruction because

Peter had a human ability to catch fish, but a human ability is not enough for Peter to have wealth. Peter encountering Jesus was now given a divine ability to get money, this is why when he caught the fish, he's getting money from the mouth of the fish and not from selling the fish, this is evidence that this is divine. The miracle is not just catching the fish and selling it to get money, it's taking money from the mouth of the fish.

In Genesis 39:2-4 (KJV), Joseph was betrayed by his brothers and was sold into slavery where he served in Potiphar's house. How does a slave prosper? How's a slave given success? God did not give him money; God gave him wealth. He was given the ability to enter the dimension called wealth. The dimension called wealth does not mean you have money because you become the money, money is a spirit and that spirit is called spirit of access because money gives you access. If you want to go to a certain country, you'll need access and you cannot go without paying for it.

Money is access. Joseph had access. People believe they'll see hundreds and thousands in their pockets and all they need is access. One of the benefits of becoming a leader is gaining access to certain resources that come with the position. As the leader of a nation, for example, there are some things that you don't have to pay for because you have automatic access.

The Relationship Between Wealth and Access

In the realm of wealth, access is the key to success. Access is worth more than money, as it is what ultimately generates wealth. Those with access are granted privileges that money alone cannot buy.

Consider individuals who have access and are recognized when they walk into a restaurant. They may not need to pay for their meal, as the access they possess can be used to generate more money for the restaurant. Therefore, businesses may take their access in exchange for what they want instead of taking their money. This proves that wealth puts you in a dimension where access is the most valuable commodity.

Joseph, for instance, did not have money, yet he was prosperous. Scripture tells us that God gave him the ability to interpret dreams, what Joseph needed was in him, God gave him Koch which made him a governor. Therefore, even if you take away all of Joseph's robe or possessions, he would still have the ability that made him prosperous. This is an excellent example of how wealth can push you into a dimension where you possess access to the resources and skills that bring prosperity.

Have you ever heard someone say they "sold their soul" to achieve fame? While it may sound like a metaphor, there's a deeper truth to it. Access is a fundamental part of success, and sometimes people are willing to do whatever it takes to attain it. Consider the example of Kylie Jenner. She became famous on Snapchat and then leveraged that audience to launch her cosmetic line. By doing so, she gained access to people's homes through the Internet, which has since generated millions of dollars. In essence, wealth is all about access.

Understanding the dimension of asking

In Mark 11:24 (KJV), the verse does not state that you will believe, but rather, that you already possess what you have received. Many people fail to attain what they want because they believe they will receive it, instead of believing that they have already received it. The verse speaks of God, where praying for something brings you to a dimension where it can be found. Entering this dimension means that you have already obtained it. The issue lies in the inability to recognise that you have entered this dimension, which determines whether you will receive it or not. Many people do not receive what they desire because they fail to realize that they have entered the place where it can be found.

To simplify, imagine that you are in a restaurant and have already ordered food. Once your order is placed, you have food, even if it has not arrived yet. If another waiter comes to take your order, you do not order again because you have already done so. Similarly, ordering repeatedly will result in being kicked out of the restaurant or dimension, as you lacked the necessary means to receive it.

Although you cannot see it in front of you, rest assured that you have received it. Many people claim to have faith, but they continue to ask the same things. If you truly believe, why would you question whether you will be healed? Remember, when you ask for anything in His name, He will provide it for you John 14:13-14 (KJV).

Understanding God's Blessings through borrowing and lending

Genesis 1:26 (KJV) and Luke 1:38 (KJV) emphasize that God wants to bless us and has given us dominion. However, we must permit Him to do so. When you lend to God, such as by giving to Him, you gain the authority to set terms with God, as described in Proverbs 22:7 (KJV). Similarly, Proverbs 19:16-18 (KJV) clarifies that pitying the poor does not equate to giving to the poor; rather, it is lending to God. The word poor here is a word called "roosh" which means needy, for example if the church needs help with equipment or a building project.

When we take pity on the needs of the church, we feel a sense of fulfilment in our contribution to the Lord's work. Giving to God is like lending to Him, and as the borrower, God is relying on us to set the terms. This is a unique opportunity to give God our terms and conditions.

Just like with any lending or borrowing, there must be terms on how and when the lent item will be returned. Even the banking system has an interest and rules that determine these terms. We are entitled to set our terms, such as when we want it returned, the type of collateral, and the level of surety. We should pray and ask for healing or assistance instead of sending letters, writing songs, or poems to God.

Let us take the time to give generously and lend to God with faith, knowing that He will honour His word and return to us that we have given.

Prayer is not just about making requests to God. It's about getting into a mindset where you can have a real conversation with Him. When you're not physically seeing God, you can still talk to Him and ask for His guidance. Start by acknowledging the Father, Son, and Holy Ghost and invite them to join you in a conversation.

When praying, it's essential to be specific. Discuss with God what's on your mind. Don't be afraid to ask for what you want but remember to be humble and trust in God's word. You can ask for blessings or deliverance, and you can also give back in return. For instance, you can give seed or build a house for God's people.

Giving is a crucial aspect of prayer, and it's something that works. When you see how much joy it brings to others, you'll understand why it's so important. If you're not seeing results, it could be that you're not giving enough. It's essential to be generous, and you'll be rewarded in return. Remember that God said Abraham is the dispenser of blessings, and so can you be.

Prayer is about building a relationship with God. Be specific and humble in your requests and be generous with your giving. Trust in God's word, and you'll see results. This is why I believe in giving because I know he that lendeth is the master over him that borrows.

When you lend to God, you can dictate precisely how you desire repayment. If it doesn't come to fruition, you may question the agreement. If you hear me pray, you might believe that something is amiss. "Lord, we discussed this. Why aren't we making progress? We must continue to progress."

Revelation is the Key to Unlocking Wealth. Money is concealed in language, much like water is contained in a bottle. Wealth is the container for money. You can't sustain money without wealth, and many individuals refuse to accept the packaging, making it difficult to maintain financial stability.

The Importance of Giving

Giving is the key to overcoming the spirit of poverty. One way of giving is by establishing an altar.

Your financial situation is determined by the level of your giving. Financial success can only be achieved if you surpass the level of your giving.

Old Money and New Money Revelation

Money is a mystical entity that can determine your financial status. If you offer a dollar, you'll be restrained to that level since other denominations of money have a higher worth. Money is a spirit that prefers to be utilised where it is most valuable.

I don't spend old money on new things. Old money refers to the funds you already possess, while new money refers to the money you haven't received yet. For instance, if I have $200,000 in my bank account and see a car worth $190,000, I haven't gained a car; I've lost $190,000. On the other hand, if I already had the $190,000 and spent it on the car, it would be an old car, not a new one. However, if I want a new car and I don't have the funds yet, I must rely on new money to pay for it instead of using the old money I already have.

There's old money and new money revelation. Those who understand the significance of sacrifice, are well aware of the importance of terminating weak offspring. Breeding weak offspring would mean continuing weak DNA, which could negatively impact the entire flock. By sacrificing weak offspring, the stronger ones are given a chance to thrive, improving the overall genetic makeup of the group.

Similarly, giving to God is like lending, where it's guaranteed to come back multiplied. As stated in Luke 6:38 (KJV), "Give, and it will be given to you. A good measure, pressed down, shaken together and running over, shall men give into your bosom." The law of physics supports this notion, where compressing and shaking something adds energy, causing it to overflow. Just like water in a kettle, when compressed and heated, it changes state and wants to shoot up.

God promises to bless us with abundance that vibrates and bombards our lives, making it too much to control. The more we give, the more we receive, and our blessings will overflow beyond our expectations.

It is said that the measure of your giving will determine the level from which you start. In other words, the amount of generosity you show will dictate how much you receive in return. You cannot surpass the highest level of your giving and thus, limit yourself to the level at which you've given.

Remember that value is not measured in numbers, but rather, where the giving comes from. Even if you can only give 1 dollar, if that 1 dollar represents all that you have, its value is immeasurable. This is exemplified in the story of the widow lady in Mark 12:41-44 (KJV). Though she gave the least, Jesus was moved by her generosity because it was all that she had.

I recall a time when I would not let go of an opportunity to give, even if it meant taking off my neck tie or belt. I refused to let an occasion go by without seizing it, even if I had nothing to give. One time, I even took off my entire suit and left only my vest and pants on. I did not do this out of a desire for others to see me as a giver, but because of my understanding of the importance of taking action. Revelation is the key that separates us and changes our lives. The more revelation you have, the more blessings you will receive. God cannot bless you beyond the level of your revelation, and the depth of your understanding of Him is what determines the level of blessings you receive.

Chapter 5:

Understanding Financial freedom

The moment we talk about freedom, we are talking about deliverance and being set free. Financial freedom is not being free to do what you want, but it is being set free from money. According to scripture 1 Timothy 6:10 (KJV), money is a master. Those who have attained financial freedom have attained mastery over money. For you to attain financial freedom, it means you have attained mastery over a master called money. Anyone who gets a hold of that revelation, that what they need is to be set free from money, that person has started the journey of attaining financial freedom. A lot of people think that to have financial freedom, they need to be delivered from poverty. Poverty does not have people in chains, money does.

Money is a Mystery

The secrets of God are not things not meant to be heard by people. God is expecting you to be a steward of the secret, but He is willing to share that secret. Whenever a secret is shared, it does not mean that the secret has been shared because what makes a secret a secret is the understanding of the secret. If I tell you a secret about what I did, without telling you why I did it, that means you have information relating to the secret, not the actual secret. Many people have gotten information about secrets but not the actual secrets from God because you need to have a relationship with God for you to receive secrets from Him.

If a teaching is presented that is meant to be a secret, it is a mystery. It is only people who understand the back end of the mystery (which means they possess the spirit behind the mystery) that will be able to understand the secret. So the people who have the spirit that is operating in a true prophet are the ones who are going to be able to receive the mystery of God. Whereas people will listen to the teaching but will not receive the secret that is in the teaching. Information can be shared with everyone, but the level of understanding is determined by the experience that one has.

When I teach, there's a level of understanding one has that is given only by the spirit.
Money is a mystery, and the things of the spirit are a mystery. It takes somebody spiritual to capture something that is hidden within that simple teaching and out of it you'll receive something greater.

Fasting vs Money Fast

When you are fasting, you are fasting from food, which means you're saying "I will punish my body such as to benefit my spirit. The moment you're fasting, it is deep. It does benefit you spiritually. You fast and your eyes are opened because you are suppressing the flesh which permits the spirit to stand out.

In a money fast, you're not denying your flesh from food, you're getting to eat what you want yet you are in a state of humility, yet you're in a state of connecting to God, yet you're in a state of attracting a certain level of light. Light is information. The information and the knowledge of God are not just knowledge. It is power, so it is an energy that you're attracting. You're receiving power from God, through this kind of fasting where you're eating everything you want to eat but God considers you to be fasting. When you go on a money fast you have enough revelation that you've gotten to a level of not fasting food but you're now fasting from money. Tithing is fasting because this money already belonged to you, but you are taking this position and saying you are fasting from it even though you need it and even though it is yours.

In Isaiah 58:6 (KJV), God is speaking to the rich, this kind of fasting can give you freedom from money. You will be set free from money, which means you're financially free and you've attained financial freedom. He's not expecting people who are financially bound to fast this kind of fast.

Gaining Mastery Over Money

In 1 Kings 17:7-9 (KJV), Prophet Elijah spoke drought into the land and was later directed by God to seek a widow's help. Despite that she expressed she didn't have enough; she was able to sustain him. However, she allowed the amount of food to determine how long she had left to live, when she should have been the one determining it. In the same way, we should control our finances, not the other way around.

Many deprive themselves of food to attract money, but this approach is flawed. Instead, we should deprive ourselves of the things we want to attract. By holding onto money while fasting from food, we give it mastery over our flesh and spirit, rather than the other way around.

Judas failed to fast from money, and as a result, he was not financially free. When presented with money, he could not resist, and money became his master. Those who refuse to be delivered from money often want to hold onto it, yet ironically, it is their top prayer request.

Money is a creation of God, and it can only be mastered by those who have gained mastery over it. To do so, we must have a certain level of spiritual understanding, which can be achieved through money fasting.

References

The Editors of Encyclopaedia Britannica. Wall Street. (2023, Nov, 8.) https://www.britannica.com/money/Wall-Street-New-York-City

Ecclesiastes 7:12 (KJV)
Matthew 2:11 (KJV)
Mark 6:12-13 (KJV)
Proverbs 23:1-2 (KJV)
Psalms 91:11-12 (KJV)
Matthew 4:5-7 (KJV)
John 20:1-18 (KJV)
Luke 7:37 (KJV)
John 12:1-8 (KJV)
Genesis 32:24-28 (KJV)
Proverbs 6:10-14 (KJV)
Proverbs 19:15 (KJV)
Matthew 13:25 (KJV)
Luke 16:13 (KJV)
Habakkuk 2:2 (KJV)
Matthew 16:4 (KJV)
Genesis 47:14 (KJV)
Ephesians 6:12 (KJV)
Deuteronomy 8:18 (KJV)
Matthew 6:24-26 (KJV)
1 Timothy 6:10 (KJV)
Matthew 6:24-26 (KJV)
Matthew 17:24-27 (KJV)
Genesis 39:2-4 (KJV)
Mark 11:24 (KJV)
Genesis 1:26 (KJV)

Luke 1:38 (KJV)
Proverbs 22:7 (KJV)
Proverbs 19:16-18 (KJV)
John 14:13-14 (KJV)
Mark 12:41-44 (KJV)

Luke 6:38 (KJV)
Timothy 6:10 (KJV)
Isaiah 58:6 (KJV)
1 Kings 17:7-9 (KJV)

Printed in the USA
CPSIA information can be obtained
at www.ICGtesting.com
LVHW070935070224
771186LV00095B/3919